D1218625

feasts of fancy

feasts of fancy

pigs in a blanket and other edible delights

Laura Cook

LONGSTREET PRESS
Atlanta, Georgia

Published by LONGSTREET PRESS, INC.,
a subsidiary of Cox Newspapers,
a division of Cox Enterprises, Inc.
2140 Newmarket Parkway
Suite 118
Marietta, Georgia 30067

Copyright © 1994 Laura Cook

Published by arrangement with Whitecap Books Ltd.,
North Vancouver, British Columbia.

1st printing 1994

Recipes by Gina Main
Edited by Elaine Jones
Cover illustration by Laura Cook
Interior design by Laura Cook

ISBN: 1-56352-181-4

Printed in China

For
skookums
and
seamoss

. . .

TABLE OF CONTENTS

𝒜NGELS ON 𝒽ORSEBACK

1	can (3.67 oz./104 g) smoked oysters, drained	1
12	slices bacon	12
	anchovy paste	

Cut bacon in half crosswise. Lightly spread inner surface of the bacon with anchovy paste. Wrap half slice of bacon around each oyster; secure with toothpick.

Place on a baking sheet in a 400°F (200°C) oven for 10-12 minutes or until bacon is crisp. Serve with salsa.

Makes 24 appetizers.

Salsa

1/2	large roasted red bell pepper	1/2
2	ripe beefsteak tomatoes	2
1/2	small firm cucumber	1/2
1	small white onion	1
1	garlic clove, minced	1
1/2 cup	chopped fresh cilantro (coriander)	125 mL
2 Tbsp.	taco or tomato sauce	25 mL
2 Tbsp.	fresh lime juice	25 mL
1 Tbsp.	rice wine vinegar	15 mL
1/2 tsp.	ground cumin	2 mL
	salt and pepper to taste	

To roast the pepper, broil it about 6 inches (15 cm) from the heat source, turning frequently until it is black all over, about 8-10 minutes. Peel the charred pepper, remove the seeds and ribs. Cut the tomatoes in half, remove the seeds and excess juice. Peel and chop the cucumber and onion. Combine all the ingredients in a food processor, mixing until fairly smooth. Chill.

Makes 2 cups (500 mL).

WILD SMOKED SALMON

Éclairs

1/2 cup	water	125 mL
1/4 cup	butter	50 mL
pinch	salt	pinch
1/2 cup	flour	125 mL
3	large eggs	3

Filling

8 oz.	whipped light cream cheese	250 g
4	slices smoked salmon	4
	finely chopped fresh dill	
1/2 cup	light sour cream	125 mL
4 oz.	black caviar	125 g

To make éclairs, place water, butter and salt in a deep saucepan and cook over medium heat until butter melts; bring to boil over high heat.

Remove from heat and add flour all at once. Beat vigorously until thoroughly blended. Return to medium heat; cook, stirring constantly, until mixture forms a ball and leaves the sides of the pan.

Remove pan from heat, cool for a moment or two, and stir in the eggs one at a time, making certain the first egg is completely incorporated before adding the next. Beat vigorously at the end.

Lightly grease a baking sheet. Pipe 2-inch (5-cm) lengths of dough onto sheet, to form 16 éclair bottoms. Top with a second strip of dough. Bake at 450°F (230°C) for 10 minutes, then reduce heat to 375°F (190°C) and bake 10 minutes more. Remove puffs from oven. Cut a slit in the side of each éclair. Cool.

Slice each éclair in half horizontally. Spread a thin layer of cream cheese on the bottom half of each éclair and lay a piece of salmon on top. Sprinkle with dill. Spread a thin layer of sour cream on the salmon. Garnish with caviar. Place éclair tops on and serve.

Makes 16 éclairs.

FIDDLEHEADS

1/2 lb.	fresh fiddlehead ferns or	250 g
	1 package frozen (10 oz./300 g)	
1/4 cup	crunchy peanut butter	50 mL
2 Tbsp.	soy sauce	25 mL
1 tsp.	sugar	5 mL
3-4 tsp.	water	15-20 mL
1	small carrot, cut into long	1
	matchsticks and blanched	
2 Tbsp.	coarsely chopped peanuts	25 mL

Wash fresh fiddlehead ferns several times in cool water. Trim the dark ends before cooking. If using frozen ones, do not thaw before cooking.

Cook the fiddleheads, uncovered, in a large amount of boiling, salted water for 4-6 minutes, or until just tender and still bright green. Chill them in cold water, drain and dry; set aside.

In a medium bowl, whisk together peanut butter, soy sauce, sugar and water. Add the fiddleheads and toss gently. Garnish with carrots and peanuts. Serve at room temperature.

Serves 4.

$\mathscr{P}$EACH $\mathscr{C}$OBBLER

4 cups	peeled and sliced ripe peaches	1 L
1/2 cup	sugar	125 mL
1 tsp.	lemon zest	5 mL
1 Tbsp.	fresh lemon juice	15 mL
1/2 tsp.	almond extract	2 mL
1 1/2 cups	flour	375 mL
4 Tbsp.	sugar, divided	50 mL
1 Tbsp.	baking powder	15 mL
1/2 tsp.	salt	2 mL
1/3 cup	shortening	75 mL
1	egg, lightly beaten	1
1/4 cup	milk	50 mL
1/4 cup	peach brandy or peach cordial	50 mL
1 cup	whipping cream, whipped	250 mL
	sifted icing sugar for dusting	
	mild-tasting edible flowers,	
	such as Johnny-jump-ups or borage	
	mint sprigs	

*P*reheat oven to 400°F (200°C). For the filling, arrange peaches in a greased 2-quart (2-L) baking dish. Sprinkle with 1/2 cup (125 mL) sugar, lemon zest and juice, and almond extract. Bake for 20 minutes.

To make the top crust, sift flour, 2 Tbsp. (25 mL) sugar, baking powder and salt together in a large bowl. Cut in shortening until mixture resembles coarse oatmeal. Combine beaten egg and milk and mix into dry ingredients until just combined.

Remove peaches from oven and quickly drop dough by large spoonfuls over surface. Sprinkle with 2 Tbsp. (25 mL) of sugar. Return to the oven for 15-20 minutes, until top is firm and golden.

Serve while still warm. Drizzle with peach brandy and top with whipped cream. Dust the top with icing sugar shaken from a sieve. Garnish with mint sprigs and edible flowers.

Serves 4-6.

CRESCENT ROLLS

1	loaf (1lb./454 g) frozen white bread dough, thawed	1
1	egg yolk	1
2 Tbsp.	milk	25 mL

Crab Filling

1/2 cup	crab meat	125 mL
2 oz.	cream cheese	60 g
	salt and pepper to taste	

Feta Cheese Filling

1/2 cup	crumbled feta cheese	125 mL
	olive oil	
	dried basil	

*E*ach filling recipe makes enough for one loaf of dough. To prepare crab filling, combine crab meat, cream cheese, salt and pepper in a food processor and process until smooth.

On a lightly floured board, roll dough into a 10-inch (25-cm) circle. Cut into 12 pie-shaped pieces. At the base of each triangle, place about 1 tsp. (5 mL) of either the crab filling or the feta cheese.

Whisk together egg yolk and milk. Carefully roll up crescent, starting at wide end. Brush tip with a little egg yolk mixture and seal point with fingers. Place on a lightly greased baking sheet and curve into a crescent shape. Cover and let rise at room temperature for about 45 minutes, until doubled in size.

Drizzle olive oil over feta cheese crescents and sprinkle with basil. Brush crab crescents with remaining egg wash.

Bake in a 375°F (190°C) oven for 20-25 minutes, until golden brown.

Makes 12 crescent rolls.

CHICKEN À LA KING

1/4 cup	butter	50 mL
1	shallot, finely chopped	1
1/3 cup	sliced mushrooms, preferably chanterelles	75 mL
1/4 cup	flour	50 mL
1 1/2 cups	chicken stock	375 mL
1/2 cup	whipping cream	125 mL
1 cup	diced cooked chicken	250 mL
2 Tbsp.	diced smoked oysters	25 mL
pinch	nutmeg	pinch
	salt	
	freshly ground pepper	
1/4 cup	diced roasted red bell pepper	50 mL
1/3 cup	cooked snow peas, cut crosswise in half	75 mL
1 Tbsp.	dry sherry	15 mL
6	baked patty shells (save pastry tops)	6

Sauté shallots in butter until translucent; add mushrooms and sauté. Stir in flour and cook, stirring, for about 2 minutes. Remove from heat and gradually stir in chicken stock and whipping cream. Cook over medium heat, stirring, until smooth and thick.

Stir in chicken, oysters, nutmeg, salt, pepper, roasted red pepper, snow peas and sherry, and heat through. Spoon mixture carefully into warm patty shells. Cut pastry tops into interesting shapes with canapé cutters and place on top. Serve at once.

Serves 6.

$\mathscr{A}$SPARAGUS $\mathscr{S}$PEARS

1 lb.	asparagus spears	500 g
1 Tbsp.	green peppercorns	15 mL
1 cup	seedless green grapes	250 mL
1/4 tsp.	salt	1 mL
3 Tbsp.	oil	45 mL
	red lettuce leaves	
	green grapes	
	cooked prawns	

Trim the tough ends from the asparagus spears. Steam asparagus for about 5-10 minutes or until tender. Chill.

Wash peppercorns and pat dry. In a food processor, combine peppercorns, grapes (skins on) and salt; process until creamy. Gradually add oil, blending until thick. Chill.

Just before serving, arrange asparagus on individual lettuce-lined plates. Garnish with grapes and prawns and drizzle with dressing. Serves 4.

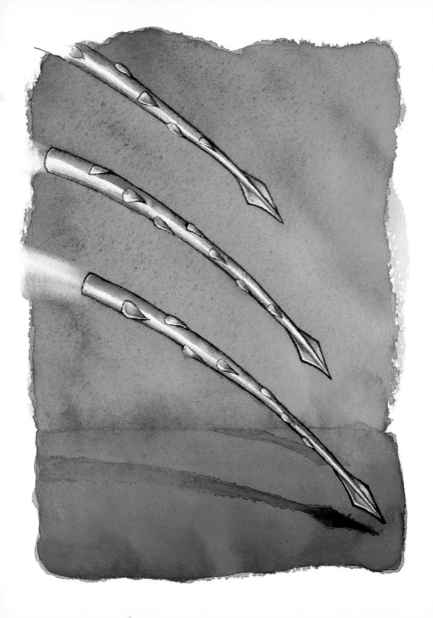

$\mathcal{D}$ATE $\mathcal{S}$QUARES

1 1/2 cups	chopped dates	375 mL
1 cup	raisins	250 mL
1 1/2 cups	boiling water	375 mL
1/2 cup	sugar	125 mL
1 tsp.	grated lemon rind	5 mL
2 Tbsp.	lemon juice	25 mL
1 cup	butter, softened	250 mL
3/4 cup	brown sugar	175 mL
1 tsp.	vanilla	5 mL
2 1/2 cups	rolled oats	625 mL
1/2 cup	flour	125 mL
1/2 cup	wheat germ	125 mL
1/2 tsp.	baking soda	2 mL
1/2 tsp.	salt	2 mL
Raspberry Coulis		
2 cups	fresh raspberries	500 mL
1 Tbsp.	sugar	15 mL
2 Tbsp.	dry red wine	25 mL

Combine dates, raisins, boiling water, sugar, lemon rind and lemon juice in a saucepan. Simmer, covered, for about 10-15 minutes or until thickened and liquid is absorbed. Cool.

Beat together butter and sugar; add vanilla. Combine oats, flour, wheat germ, baking soda and salt. Using a pastry blender, cut into butter mixture. Press half of the oat mixture over the bottom of a greased 9-inch (23-cm) square pan. Spread with cooled filling. Sprinkle with remaining oats mixture.

Bake in 350°F (180°C) oven for 30-35 minutes. Cool.

Boil coulis ingredients together for 3 minutes over medium heat, then push the mixture through a fine sieve and chill.

To serve, place some of the coulis on an individual dessert plate and top with a warm date square.

Makes 9 3-inch (7-cm) squares.

Deviled Eggs

6	eggs	6
1/4 cup	imported black olives (such as Kalamata), pitted	50 mL
4	imported green olives (such as Sicilian), pitted	4
2	anchovy fillets	2
1	garlic clove	1
1 Tbsp.	capers, thoroughly drained	15 mL
1 Tbsp.	oil-packed tuna, drained	15 mL
1 Tbsp.	lemon juice	15 mL
1/2 cup	fresh basil leaves, rinsed and patted dry	125 mL
2 Tbsp.	olive oil	25 mL
2 Tbsp.	mayonnaise	25 mL

Place eggs in a saucepan and add enough water to cover eggs. Cover saucepan and bring rapidly just to boiling. Remove pan from heat and let eggs stand 15-20 minutes in the hot water. Cool immediately and thoroughly in cold running water.

Combine black and green olives, anchovy fillets, garlic, capers, tuna, lemon juice and basil in a food processor. Process until smooth. With motor still running, gradually add oil to make a thick, fluffy sauce. Blend in the mayonnaise.

Cut eggs in half, lengthwise, and scoop out yolks. Press yolks through a sieve and fold into filling. Pipe mixture into egg whites.

Optional Garnishes
- *red or black caviar*
- *sprigs of fresh dill or watercress*
- *smoked salmon*
- *baby shrimp*
- *crumbled cooked bacon*

Makes 12 deviled eggs.

CORNED BEEF

2 lbs.	corned beef	1 kg
1/2 cup	Seville orange marmalade	125 mL
2 Tbsp.	Dijon mustard	25 mL
1 Tbsp.	brown sugar	15 mL

Place corned beef in a large pot and cover with boiling water. Bring to a boil, reduce heat, cover partially and simmer as slowly as possible for about 2 hours, or until very tender when tested with a fork.

In a small bowl, mix together marmalade, mustard and sugar.

When meat is cooked, remove from pot and drain. Place meat on an ovenproof serving dish. Coat thoroughly with the marmalade mixture.

Place corned beef in a 350°F (180°C) oven. Bake for 20-30 minutes, or until glaze is crisp and brown. Serve hot or at room temperature.

Serves 4-6.

ᔍUMMER ᔍQUASH

6	small summer squash (such as zucchini)	6
1/4 cup	butter, melted	50 mL
1	clove garlic, minced	1
1/4 cup	freshly grated Parmesan cheese	50 mL
1 Tbsp.	chopped fresh parsley	15 mL
1 tsp.	dry savory, crumbled	5 mL

Wash squash; remove ends and cut in half. Cut each half lengthwise into 1/8-inch (2-mm) slices, leaving about 3/4 inch (2 cm) of squash intact at one end. Steam until tender crisp, about 5 minutes.

Place summer squash on a flat surface and press to spread sliced end open like a fan. Place squash in a greased baking dish. In a small bowl, combine melted butter, garlic, Parmesan cheese, parsley and savory. Spread over summer squash fans. Bake, uncovered, in a 400°F (200°C) oven for 15 minutes or until heated through.

Serves 6.

Banana Loaf

2	large ripe bananas, mashed	2
3/4 cup	sugar	175 mL
2	eggs	2
1/2 cup	oil	125 mL
1 1/4 cups	flour	300 mL
1 tsp.	baking soda	5 mL
1/3 cup	sliced toasted almonds	75 mL
2 oz.	semi-sweet chocolate, grated	60 g

Preheat oven to 350°F (180°C). Beat together bananas, sugar, eggs and oil. Sift together flour and baking soda; add to wet ingredients. Fold in almonds and semi-sweet chocolate.

Pour into a greased loaf pan. Bake in 350°F (180°C) oven for 50-60 minutes or until a tester inserted in center comes out clean.

Makes 1 loaf (24 thin or 16 thick slices).

PIGS IN A BLANKET

1 lb.	sweet Italian sausage	500 g
1/4 cup	chopped Italian parsley (cilantro)	50 mL
1 tsp.	each salt and pepper	5 mL
1/2 cup	chopped pistachio nuts	125 mL
1/2 tsp.	cayenne pepper	2 mL
1 Tbsp.	butter	15 mL
1 Tbsp.	olive oil	15 mL
2	shallots, finely chopped	2
2	cloves garlic, minced	2
1	package (14 oz./400 g) frozen puff pastry, thawed	1
1	egg yolk	1
2 tsp.	cold water	10 mL

Mix together sausage, parsley, salt, pepper, pistachio nuts and cayenne. In a small frying pan, melt butter with the olive oil and cook shallots and garlic until softened. Add to sausage mixture and mix well.

Cut pastry in half. Roll each half into an 18- x 6-inch (45- x 15-cm) rectangle. Shape sausage mixture into 2 rolls, about 1 inch (2.5 cm) each in diameter. Place along long edges of pastry. Roll up jelly-roll style. Dampen edges of pastry and seal. Place roll seam-side-down on a board; chill 15 minutes. With a sharp knife, cut roll into 1-inch (2.5-cm) lengths.

On a parchment-lined baking sheet, place rolls seam-side-down. Beat together egg yolk and cold water and brush over tops of rolls. Bake in a 450°F (230°C) oven for 10 minutes. Reduce heat to 375°F (190°C) and bake for another 15 minutes, or until golden brown.

Makes 24 rolls.

PORTERHOUSE STEAK

4	porterhouse steaks	4
1/4 cup	cracked black pepper	50 mL
4	cloves garlic, minced	4
4	bay leaves	4
1 Tbsp.	chopped fresh rosemary	15 mL
3/4 cup	dry red wine	175 mL
2 Tbsp.	olive oil	25 mL
1 Tbsp.	red wine vinegar	15 mL
1 cup	beef stock	250 mL
1/4 cup	cornstarch	50 mL
1/4 cup	water	50 mL
	salt	
	freshly ground pepper	
1 cup	blue cheese, crumbled	250 mL

Rub the porterhouse steaks with cracked black pepper and garlic, and place in a non-aluminum container. Add the bay leaves, rosemary, red wine, oil and vinegar. Cover and refrigerate overnight, turning the steaks several times.

Remove the meat from the marinade and dry steaks. Strain the marinade into a saucepan and boil over medium heat until it is reduced by half. Add beef stock to the marinade mixture.

Mix the cornstarch and water together, whisk into sauce. Reduce heat to medium-low; simmer for 5-7 minutes until thick.

Season steaks with salt and pepper. Barbecue or broil steaks. Remove the steaks to a warmed platter and cover.

Remove the sauce from the heat and whisk in 3/4 cup (175 mL) crumbled blue cheese, stirring until smooth. To serve, pour sauce over steaks and garnish with remaining crumbled blue cheese.

Serves 4.

SHOESTRING POTATOES

4	peeled potatoes, preferably	4
	Yukon Gold or russet	
1/4 cup	olive oil	50 mL
2 Tbsp.	melted butter	25 mL
6	sprigs fresh thyme	6
	or 2 tsp. (10 mL) dried	
	salt	
	freshly ground pepper	

Cut the potatoes lengthwise into thin, shoestring pieces; then cut the pieces in half crosswise. Put the potatoes in a large non-aluminum bowl filled with cold water until ready to use. Drain and dry well on paper towels.

Toss potatoes with oil and melted butter and spread out on a baking sheet or dark roasting pan. Lay thyme sprigs over potatoes. Bake for 15-20 minutes in a 400°F (200°C) oven, turning occasionally, until potatoes are brown and crisp on all sides.

Remove from oven, discard thyme stems (the leaves will have fallen off), and season with salt and pepper. Serve immediately.

Serves 4-6.

MINCEMEAT TARTS

1 cup	mincemeat	250 mL
2 tsp.	grated orange rind	10 mL
12	2 1/2-in./6-cm tart shells	12
2	eggs	2
1	can (14 oz./396 g)	1
	sweetened condensed milk	
1 tsp.	cinnamon	5 mL
1/2 tsp.	nutmeg	2 mL
1/2 tsp.	ginger	2 mL
1/4 tsp.	salt	1 mL
1	can (16 oz./453 g) pumpkin	1
1/2 cup	whipping cream, whipped	125 mL
	orange rind slivers	

Preheat oven to 425°F (220°C). Combine mincemeat and grated orange rind and divide among the tart shells.

In a large bowl, beat eggs until frothy. Stir in condensed milk, cinnamon, nutmeg, ginger, salt and pumpkin. Mix well until smooth. Pour over mincemeat layer in tart shells. If using homemade pastry, decorate tops with leftover pastry shapes.

Bake tarts for 10-15 minutes at 425°F (220°C), or until a knife inserted comes out clean. When cool, pipe whipped cream rosettes and garnish with orange rind slivers.

Makes 12 tarts.

MUSHROOM CAPS

12	medium-sized mushroom caps	12
1 Tbsp.	olive oil	15 mL
1 Tbsp.	butter	15 mL
1/3 cup	finely chopped onion	75 mL
2 Tbsp.	coarsely chopped walnut meats	25 mL
1	clove garlic, minced	1
1/4 cup	frozen chopped spinach	50 mL
1/2 cup	asiago cheese, grated	125 mL
1/2 cup	Gruyère cheese, grated	125 mL
2 Tbsp.	minced fresh dill	25 mL
	salt and pepper to taste	

Thoroughly defrost spinach and squeeze dry. Remove stems from mushroom caps and set stems aside for another use. Wipe caps.

In a small skillet, heat olive oil and butter. Add the onion and cook over medium heat, covered, until tender and lightly coloured, about 10-15 minutes.

Add walnuts and garlic to onion mixture; cook 1 minute. Add spinach and cook for another 5 minutes, stirring constantly. Remove from heat; cool slightly. Stir in cheeses, dill, and salt and pepper to taste.

Arrange mushroom caps cavity-side-up in an ovenproof serving dish. Divide the spinach-walnut mixture among the mushroom caps.

Bake in the upper third of a 400°F (200°C) oven for 8-10 minutes, or until the filling is browned and the mushrooms are completely heated through. Serve immediately.

Makes 12 stuffed caps.

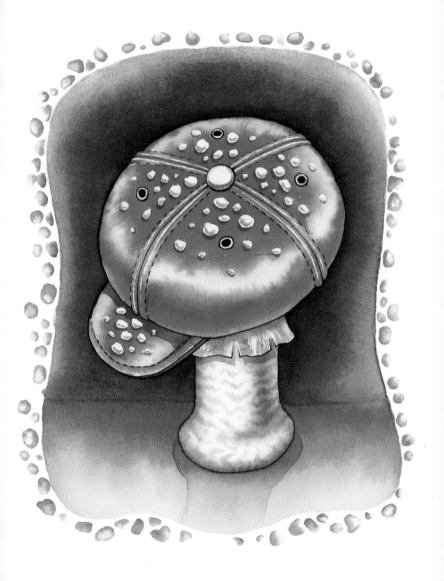

RACK OF LAMB

3/4 cup	olive oil	175 mL
1/4 cup	red wine vinegar	50 mL
1/4 cup	chopped fresh parsley	50 mL
1 tsp.	Dijon mustard	5 mL
1 tsp.	salt	5 mL
1 tsp.	crumbled dry thyme	5 mL
2	bay leaves, crumbled	2
2	racks of lamb, with 6 ribs each	2
3	garlic cloves, slivered	3
1/2 cup	dry red wine	125 mL
1/3 cup	finely chopped shallots	75 mL
1 cup	lamb or chicken stock	250 mL
	cracked pepper	
1/3 cup	olive oil	75 mL
1/2 cup	unsalted butter, cut into 8 pieces	125 mL
	salt and freshly ground pepper	

*M*ix *together 3/4 cup (175 mL) oil, vinegar, parsley, mustard, salt, thyme and bay leaves. Cut small slits in lamb; press garlic slivers into slits. In a large glass baking dish, cover the lamb with the marinade. Refrigerate overnight, turning occasionally. Boil wine and shallots in a heavy saucepan until liquid is reduced to 2 Tbsp. (25 mL). Add stock and boil until liquid is reduced to 2/3 cup (150 mL). Set aside.*

Preheat oven to 450°F (230°C). Remove lamb from marinade; pat dry; rub with cracked pepper. In a large roasting pan over medium heat, brown lamb racks in 1/3 cup (75 mL) oil. Roast lamb in oven until rare, about 35-40 minutes.

Pour off any fat from roasting pan. Add reduced stock to pan and bring to a boil, scraping up any browned bits. Over low heat whisk in butter, 1 piece at a time. Season with salt and pepper. Serve sauce with lamb.

Serves 4-6.

Wax Beans

1	carrot, peeled	1
1/2 lb.	wax beans, trimmed	250 g
2 Tbsp.	unsalted butter	25 mL
1	garlic clove, minced	1
	red bell pepper strips	
	lemon peel strips (optional)	
	salt	
	white pepper	

Using a vegetable peeler, scrape 4 long strips from carrot. Add carrot strips to a saucepan of boiling water; boil until limp, about 30 seconds. Cool carrot strips.

Steam wax beans about 5-10 minutes, or until tender-crisp. Cool under cold running water.

Gather 8-12 wax beans in a bundle. Wrap 1 carrot strip about bundle and tie in a knot. Trim carrot ends if necessary. Repeat with remaining wax beans and carrot strips. The bundles can be refrigerated, covered, for up to 8 hours.

Steam bundles until heated through. In a small frying pan, melt butter; sauté garlic for 30 seconds. Place bundles on platter; brush with butter mixture. Garnish with red pepper and lemon peel strips, if desired. Season with salt and pepper to taste.

Serves 4.

FRUIT COCKTAIL

1 cup	pineapple chunks (reserve juice)	250 mL
1/2 cup	chopped dried apricots	125 mL
1/4 cup	raisins	50 mL
1	mango	1
2 cups	sliced strawberries	500 mL
1 cup	seedless green grapes	250 mL
2 cups	champagne, chilled	500 mL

Put juice from pineapple in a measuring cup and add enough water to make 1 cup (250 mL). Simmer dried apricots and raisins in the pineapple juice and water mixture for 15 minutes. Chill.

Peel mango; cut into bite-sized pieces, discarding large flat pit. In a large bowl combine dried fruit mixture, mango, strawberries and grapes.

To serve, fill 6 stemmed glasses with fruit mixture. Fill with champagne.

Serves 6.